DATE DUE

DEMCO 38-297

NBA
CHAMPIONS

Doug Marx

BASKETBALL
HEROES

The Rourke Corporation, Inc.
Vero Beach, Florida 32964

The Rourke Corporation, Inc.
P.O. Box 3328, Vero Beach, FL 32964

Marx, Doug.
    NBA Champions / by Doug Marx.
        p. cm. - (Basketball heroes)
    Includes bibliographical references (p. 46) and index.
    Summary: Traces the history of professional basketball's championship playoffs since the NBA's first season in 1949-1950.
    ISBN 0-86593-160-7
    1. National Basketball Association—History—Juvenile literature. [1. National Basketball Association—History. 2. Basketball—History.] I. Title. II. Series.
GV885.59.N37M37 1992
796.323'64'0973—dc20
                                                  92-9481
                                                      CIP
                                                        AC

Series Editor: Gregory Lee
Editor: Marguerite Aronowitz
Book design and production: The Creative Spark, San Clemente, CA
Cover photograph: Ken Levine

Contents

Champions Of Today
And Yesterday   5

The 1960s   11

The 1970s   19

The 1980s   27

The 1990s   37

NBA Champions   43

Glossary   45

Bibliography   46

Index   48

One of the most exciting matchups in NBA finals history pitted Michael Jordan and the Chicago Bulls against Magic Johnson and the Los Angeles Lakers.

Champions Of Today And Yesterday

It is June 1991. Sportswriters around the country are having a field day. The Los Angeles Lakers are meeting the Chicago Bulls head-on in a National Basketball Association (NBA) championship series that everyone is calling the matchup of the century. The championship is like the World Series or Super Bowl of pro basketball, and two of the finest players to ever set foot on a hardwood court will help decide whose team is best: Magic Johnson and Michael Jordan.

Although the face-off between Magic and Michael is a classic, it is only one of many in NBA championship history. In the 1980s, Magic and the Boston Celtics' Larry Bird went at it three times in tournament play, amazing the fans. In the early 1970s, two big centers—Willis Reed of the Knicks and Wilt Chamberlain of the Lakers— knocked heads under the hoop. Later that decade, the Celtics big man, Dave Cowens, would face Kareem Abdul-Jabbar.

Although such individual matchups add to the excitement of the NBA finals, there is much more to the event than that. Basketball is a team game, and year-in, year-out, the finals are the showcase where the finest teams in the NBA get a chance to show their talents. For example, in the 1960s the Celtics and their center Bill Russell won seven championships. It did not make any difference who was matched up against them. And who can forget the 1974-75 series when the underdog Golden State Warriors, led by pass-master Rick Barry, demolished the Washington Bullets—a team that boasted such stars as Elvin Hayes, Wes Unseld, and Phil Chenier?

Two years later another team-oriented squad, the Portland Trail Blazers led by Bill Walton, upset the Philadelphia 76ers, whose hopes were carried by superstar Julius "Dr. J" Erving.

This book is a history of the NBA championships from their beginnings in 1950 to the "Magic and Michael" show of 1991. Taking a year-by-year look at the best pro basketball has to offer, we will discover how such dynasties as the Boston teams of the 1960s and the Lakers of the 1980s developed. In 40 years there has been a lot of highlights, and a lot of amazing players who provided the magic and the drama.

The First Decade

Back in 1891, James A. Naismith, a physical education teacher at a small college in Springfield, Massachusetts, wanted to invent a game his students could play indoors during the winter. The gym was too

There would have been no NBA champions without Dr. James Naismith, the founder of the game of basketball.

small for soccer or rugby, and playing lacrosse indoors—with those long-handled rackets—was just plain dangerous. An entirely different game was needed. Naismith, the "Father of Basketball," nailed a peach basket to a 10-foot-high gym balcony, tossed a soccer ball into it, and the game of basketball was born. Along with baseball and football, it soon became one of the most popular sports in the United States.

Everyone played it. Women's teams were formed right from the beginning. The peach basket was soon replaced by a steel hoop with a net, but not before metal baskets with *closed* bottoms were tried! In the 1920s and 1930s, promoters put chicken wire around the court so the ball could not fly into the crowd.

After earlier efforts to build a professional league failed, the National Basketball Association was formed in 1949. It was a success. Fans flocked to see the finest players in the game take their positions on one of the league's 17 teams. And each spring they were treated to a showdown between the best: The NBA Championship series. These games were classics right from the start.

The first NBA Championship was played in the spring of 1950 between the Minneapolis Lakers and the Syracuse Nationals. The Lakers eventually moved to Los Angeles and had championship years with Kareem Abdul-Jabbar at center. But Jabbar was not the first superstar center to play for the Lakers. Over 40 years ago, they had big George Mikan, a Hall of Famer the Associated Press voted "the greatest basketball star of the first half of the 20th century."

The Lakers were favored, and they beat the Nationals 4-2, but not without a struggle. In fact, the series was marred by several fistfights that broke out among the players. In Game 6 of a seesaw series, played before nearly 10,000 hometown fans, Mikan turned in one of his finest performances. At six-feet, ten-inches tall, he carried a 27.4 point average into the game. After dropping 40 in the bucket that night, he led his team to a 110-95 victory. One hundred point games were quite rare in those days. Mikan had led the way to seven others that opening NBA year, turning in a 51-point game to boot.

Basketball was a slower game then. For example, players did not have a 24-second clock pushing them to hurry and shoot. Mikan's 51 points seemed superhuman. The clock became a part of the game a year after he retired. Before turning in his uniform at the end of the 1953-54 season, Mikan led his team to three more championships.

The 1950-51 trophy went to the Rochester Royals. Having beaten the Lakers in the playoffs, the Royals took on the New York Knickerbockers, and again the series was a classic. Tied at three games apiece, the championship went right down to the wire in the seventh game. A scrappy, back-and-forth battle came to a 75-75 tie with less than 30 seconds to play. A foul was whistled and Royals' guard Bob Davies went to the line. He calmly swished two *free throws*, giving the Royals their glory. A last-second *lay-up* by the Royals' Jack Coleman iced the game at 79-75.

Red Holzman, who would go on to coach world champion Knickerbocker teams in the 1960s, was a key player in the Royals' victory. On the Knicks' side was Nat "Sweetwater" Clifton. Clifton had come from the Harlem Globetrotters, and was one of the first black players to break basketball's "color line."

The Syracuse Nationals lost to Minneapolis again in Mikan's last year. But things changed in 1954-55 when they won it all. The following season, the Philadelphia Warriors, for many years a playoff contender, got their first chance at an NBA Championship where they defeated the Fort Wayne Pistons.

Then it happened. A season to remember: 1956-57. The Boston Celtics, who continually floundered in playoff action, made it to the finals and beat the St. Louis Hawks. The Celtics would go on to ten more NBA Championship series in a row, losing only twice, and winning eight years in a row! After their streak ended, leaving the 1966-67 season to Philadelphia and San Francisco, they bounced back to take the crown the next two years.

Outstanding players like John Havlicek—along with Bob Cousy, Bill Russell, and Boston coach Red Auerbach—helped the Celtics dominate the NBA Championships during the 1960s.

The 1960s

In 1950, when the Lakers and the Royals were tearing up the league, the Celtics were losing— badly. Then they hired Arnold "Red" Auerbach as coach. In future years, the Celtics would sign such Hall-of-Fame players as Bob Cousy, Bill Russell, Tom Heinsohn, and John Havlicek. But no one was more important to the success of the Celtics than Auerbach. He put a playoff team together within a couple of years and brought a title to Boston in the spring of 1957. For the next 16 years, he presided over a pro basketball dynasty whose winning ways may never be equaled.

Just as Mikan became the first big modern center, towering over his opponents, guard Bob Cousy became a big little man for the Celtics. A hair over six-feet tall, he redefined the guard position and role of "little man" in the sport. He was nicknamed "Cooz." He became one of the finest passers the game has ever seen, and led the NBA in assists for eight seasons in a row! He

---

NBA Trivia

Q: Who has scored the most three-point field goals in playoff action?
A: Michael Cooper, with 121.

Q: Who has the most assists in playoff action?
A: Magic Johnson leads in both career highs (with 2,320) and single-game record with 24.

Q: Who scored the most points in a four-game NBA Championship series?
A: Rick Barry, Golden State vs. Washington, with 118.

was also the first to dribble the ball behind his back. This superb shooter brought so much magic to the court that fans came out in droves to see him.

Auerbach and Cousy alone could not bring a title to Boston. But then Tom Heinsohn was signed in 1956, promptly taking Rookie of the Year honors. And then Bill Sharman, another hot hand. And then Bill Russell, who many consider the finest center ever to play the game—Kareem Abdul-Jabbar included. Russell is certainly the finest defensive center in NBA history. Finally, the Celtics had a winning coach and a powerhouse team. Winning 11 of 13 championships between 1957 and 1969, they amazed the sports world.

The Celtics' first championship was one of the most thrilling. The St. Louis Hawks, led by Hall-of-Famer Bob Pettit, battled Boston to a 3-3 tie. In the deciding seventh game, Boston opened the fourth quarter with an 83-77 lead. The Hawks went on a tear, scoring nine straight points during one stretch. With six seconds left on the clock, the Celtics were hanging on to a skimpy 103-101 lead. Russell fouled Pettit, who cooly sank both his free throws, sending the game into *overtime*.

With each team trading baskets, the first overtime ended in a 113-113 tie! The fans were going crazy. A second overtime went back-and-forth as well. The lead changed hands with every shot. Boston was ahead 124-123 with just 23 seconds left on the clock. A free throw bumped the lead to two points with one second left in the game. The Hawks' Alex Hannum took an inbounds pass and fired it down court, where Pettit waited to catch it off the backboard and make the shot. Catch it he did, but the shot bounced off the rim and the Celtics had their championship.

St. Louis got its revenge the next season, downing Boston in a six-game series. But that would be the last

One of the Celtics' great opponents was Elgin Baylor and the Los Angeles Lakers, who lost time after time to the great Boston dynasty.

time for eight years that anyone could take the title away from the Celtics.

The First Dynasty

In the spring of 1959, the Celtics swept the Lakers 4-0, despite the skills of Elgin Baylor, who was the new star in Minneapolis since Mikan had retired.

Defeating the Hawks again in the following two years, Boston went after its fourth straight championship in 1962, this time against a Laker team

Red Auerbach (left) and Bob Cousy (right) were a championship combination. Auerbach assembled and coached a dynasty, and Cousy was the game's first great guard.

that had moved to Los Angeles. Baylor now had a couple of hot-shooting teammates, Frank Selvy and Tommy Hawkins. But the Lakers were not enough to stop the Celtics. They managed to stay in it to the last, but lost a tense, hard-fought seventh game 110-107. Boston repeated the feat again in 1963, beating the Lakers for their fifth straight title. At the end of the season Bob Cousy retired, ending a magnificent 13-year career. He recorded a lifetime-leading 6,959 assists and scored 16,950 points.

Boston lost one of the game's superior playmakers in Cousy, but they kept winning championships anyway. They just found Hall of Famer Sam Jones to take his place. The San Francisco Warriors were the next victim in a quick 4-1 series. And the year after that, 1965, they kept right on winning, destroying the Lakers once more. They crushed Los Angeles 4-1, routing them in the final game 129-96.

Seven straight NBA championships! When would it end? They did it one more time, but not before the Lakers ran the series out to a 3-3 tie, forcing the final game. Bill Russell led the Celtics with 25 points and an amazing 32 rebounds.

The road to that eighth crown had not been smooth for the Boston club. The team placed second in the Eastern League, behind the Philadelphia 76ers. The Sixers were led by Wilt "The Stilt" Chamberlain, whose matchups with Russell gave the game of basketball some of its most spectacular moments. Boston beat Philadelphia handily in the semifinals that spring of 1966, but Chamberlain and the Sixers would be ready and waiting the following season.

With nine championship seasons to his credit and 1,037 Celtic victories, Red Auerbach retired. Bill Russell became the new player-coach, the first black man to coach any professional sport. But his team would not

*The 1960s came to a close with a fitting matchup of the titans:
Boston's Bill Russell (6) and Los Angeles' Wilt Chamberlain (13).*

finish 1967 with an NBA title. Wilt and the Sixers would see to that. In the Eastern Division it was another one-two, Sixer-Celtic finish like the year before. This time the Celtics went down 4-1 in the playoffs, and their streak came to an end. Philadelphia went on to the NBA Championship and defeated San Francisco in a 4-2 series.

The Rivalry Continues

Some fans may have thought that the Celtic dynasty had come to an end, but they were mistaken. Besides Russell, the Celtics had John "Hondo" Havlicek, a clutch-shooting Hall of Famer known as the best sixth man in the game. Boston won both the 1967-68 and 1968-69 championships, when they faced their old enemy the Lakers. Try as they might, the Lakers just could not win. These were hard-fought championships, but the real action seemed to be in the playoffs, where Russell and Chamberlain went nose-to-nose. At any rate, the Lakers lost the first battle four games to two. But they took the 1968-69 rematch to the seventh game before losing the championship to their rivals yet again.

The Lakers had superstars Elgin Baylor and Jerry West, but they were not enough to stop the Celtics. Looking back over Boston's 11 championships in 13 years, Los Angeles had been the runner-up seven times! They would lose yet another chance at the crown to the Knicks in 1970. Finally in March 1972, they took their first NBA title since moving to Los Angeles. But that is another decade, a decade in which the Celtics, too, made championship appearances—but their days as a dynasty were over.

Both the Knicks, with the likes of Dave DeBusschere (22), and the Golden State Warriors with Rick Barry (24), won NBA Championships in the 1970s.

The 1970s

The new decade called for a different team to capture the fans' hearts, and that team was the New York Knickerbockers—the Knicks. During the late 1960s, coach Red Holzman was grooming his future champions. Willis Reed was a do-it-all center who pounded the boards. Bill Bradley, today a U.S. Senator, had one of the best jump shots in the game. Dick Arnett's long bombs left everybody breathless. Forward Dave DeBusschere gave Reed plenty of extra rebound muscle, and had a soft shot to go with it. Lastly, there was Walt Frazier, whose flashy shooting and ball-stealing would take him straight to the Hall of Fame.

The Knicks got off to a 17-1 start, which made fans and sportswriters alike take notice. Then they proceeded to win their next 18 games in a row. Everybody was watching the Knicks. They won all season long, taking their perfect outside shooting game straight to the NBA finals.

One of the oldest teams in the league, the Knicks had never won a championship. Their opponent, the Los Angeles Lakers, had lost so many championships over the last 20 years that it seemed only natural they should lose again. Elgin Baylor and Jerry West continued to be a deadly combination, and Wilt Chamberlain was now wearing a Laker uniform. Still, they lost. But not before going nose-to-nose with the Knicks right down to the last seconds of the seventh game.

This was a tight, tension-filled championship series with two overtime games. New York came from behind to win the opener, then the Lakers picked up a two-point win to tie the series. Basketball fans still talk about Game 3. The Lakers had blown a big lead, and were behind by two points with three seconds left. Chamberlain, inbounding the ball from under the Knicks' basket, threw it to West who was standing a few feet outside the free-throw line. With Willis Reed's hand in his face, West turned and pumped a miraculous 63-foot jump shot that went in and tied the game at the buzzer!

Unfortunately, the Lakers could not keep the momentum. The Knicks came right back in overtime to win which gave them a 2-1 lead in the series. The very next night, with this nightmare overtime loss behind them, the Lakers once again battled the Knicks to a tie game at the end of regulation play. Another overtime game! Wanting more defensive height, Laker Coach Joe Mullaney put in a young, unknown substitute named John Tresvant, whose hustle inspired the Lakers to defeat the Knicks 121-115. The series was tied.

In Game 5, with an injured Willis Reed on the bench, the Knicks dug deep and, with some fine ball-stealing by Frazier, once again went ahead in this seesaw series. The Lakers, weakened but not yet defeated, came right back in Game 6 to knot the series one more time at 3-3.

Then, in the seventh and final game, Reed returned to action. His offensive game was off, but he was able to stop Chamberlain, and the Knicks rolled to a 113-99 victory. Frazier, with a clutch 36 points, played the finest game of his career. His exceptional performance helped the Knicks win their first NBA Championship.

20

*Walt Frazier played with Hall of Fame style during the Knicks'
appearances in the NBA finals.*

The Abdul-Jabbar Era

The Knicks hoped to repeat in the 1970-71 season,
but the Milwaukee Bucks and a young center named
Lew Alcindor had different plans. Walking away with
the Rookie of the Year award in the previous season,
Alcindor now teamed up with the veteran playmaker
Oscar Robertson. Together they led the Bucks to the
crown.

Alcindor, known as "Mr. Inside," and Robertson,
known as "Mr. Outside," led the Bucks to a 66-16

regular season finish before shutting down the Baltimore Bullets 4-0 in the finals. Robertson was a future Hall of Famer who, with this championship, was winding down a fantastic career. Alcindor was just getting started. The basketball world would hear a lot more from him. When he adopted the Muslim faith one year later, he changed his name to Kareem Abdul-Jabbar.

The Lakers, At Last!

Just as winning streaks have to end, so too do losing streaks. The 1971-72 NBA season would finally be the Lakers' year. First, with Chamberlain and West leading the way, they turned in a record-setting 69-13 season. As if that were not enough, they also turned in a 33-game winning streak!

Tearing right through their playoff opponents, the Lakers kept their winning ways into the finals, out-dueling the Knicks 3-1 after four games. The Knicks were not about to quit, but Chamberlain and West were determined to win that fifth game. And they did, in style. Coming off a season in which he had scored his 30,000th point, Chamberlain bagged another 24 in the final game. West, playing with a sorely sprained wrist, poured in 33 more, and the Lakers had the victory, 114-100.

The Lakers hoped to repeat their title-winning act in 1972-73, once again against the Knicks, but it was not to be. The Knicks turned right around and whipped Chamberlain, West and Company 4-1, reversing their defeat of the year before.

Then it was Boston's turn again. Sportswriters called it "A Matter of Celtic Pride." With a new young center named Dave Cowens picking up where Bill Russell left off, and ageless veteran John Havlicek providing guidance and offensive punch, the Celtics downed the Milwaukee Bucks, 4-3. Game 6 was the best—another double-overtime effort. The two extra periods saw the lead change 12 times. Havlicek said that game had the best defense he had ever seen by two teams at the same time.

Everything seemed to be going Boston's way when Havlicek cooly canned a baseline jumper with three seconds on the clock, giving the Celtics a 101-100 lead. But then Abdul-Jabbar, with the poise that made him famous, calmly dropped a 15-foot hook shot that tied the series at 3-3. In Game 7, with the Bucks double- and triple-teaming Havlicek, Cowens got the hot hand, and the Bucks went under 102-87.

Boston's Back

After the Golden State Warriors with superstar Rick Barry swept the Washington Bullets in a 4-0 upset (1974-75 championship series), Boston was right back at it the following year. The Phoenix Suns had made it to their first title opportunity, but fans were talking about another Celtic dynasty. Boston did eventually dump the Suns 4-2, but not before struggling through an incredible three-overtime fifth game on their home court.

Game 5 of that 1975-76 Boston-Phoenix series might be the greatest NBA Championship game of all time. With regulation play ending in a 95-95 stalemate, the first overtime closed at 101-101. The Boston fans were coming unglued. Toward the end of the second overtime, the Suns pulled ahead 110-109. But Havlicek came right back with a shot that put the Celtics ahead by a single point.

Fans mobbed the floor. Phoenix players had to run for cover. A near-riot ensued. When the dust had settled, a referee announced that the game was not over—there was still one second left on the clock! The Suns did not

Big Bill Walton led the surprising Portland Trail Blazers to their
first NBA Championship in 1977.

have any timeouts left, but coach Paul Westphal called one anyway, which earned him a technical. Boston made the free throw and moved to a 112-110 lead. But Phoenix still had that one second to put the ball in play at midcourt. Garfield Heard took the inbounds pass and put up a jumper that swished in, taking the game into its third overtime! Boston hung on to win 128-126, returning to Phoenix for Game 6 and a championship victory.

The last half of the 1970s had its share of excitement as well. After that Boston-Phoenix super series, the Portland Trail Blazers, led by center Bill Walton, dropped the Philadelphia 76ers 4-2. Walton, whose career was cut short by injuries, was one of the finest passing centers in the game. He led a famous UCLA team coached by Hall-of-Famer John Wooden that dominated college basketball in the '70s.

Walton's regular-season and semifinal matchups with Abdul-Jabbar were basketball at its best. Down 2-0 against the Sixers, the Blazers staged one of the greatest comebacks in championship history, winning the next four games in a row.

Washington and Seattle traded championships in 1977-78 and 1978-79, with the Bullets winning the first meeting, 4-3, and the Sonics then getting their revenge, 4-1.

The spring of 1980 would find the Lakers once again in the thick of things. Abdul-Jabbar had a new teammate named Earvin "Magic" Johnson, and the Lakers were ready to roll.

Dr. J—the great Julius Erving—stormed many a basket on his way to an NBA championship for the Philadelphia 76ers in 1983.

The 1980s

F rom the spring of 1980 to the spring of 1989, the NBA Championships could almost be described in one word: Lakers. The Celtics, however, did their share to make the games exciting in that decade. Los Angeles appeared in eight of the spring classics, and Boston in six. They squared-off against one another four times, providing some of the most memorable basketball in the game's history. Houston, Philadelphia, and Detroit made appearances in the finals, but usually only to play fall-guy to the Lakers or Celts.

The Lakers were determined to win. It was as if all those playoff losses during the 1960s were still nagging at their team memory. They started their comeback in May of 1980, facing Philadelphia. In Game 5 Abdul-Jabbar sprained an ankle. Starting at center in Game 6 was six-foot, nine-inch point guard Magic Johnson! Abdul-Jabbar had led the Lakers to a 3-2 edge, and then Magic took over, laughing all the way. Before the night was out, Magic had 42 points, 15 rebounds, seven assists, three steals, and a blocked shot. With or without Abdul-Jabbar, Julius Erving and the Sixers did not have a chance. The final score was 123-107.

In 1980-81, Abdul-Jabbar was back in fine form, but Magic went down with a severe knee injury, and the Lakers struggled. The division title went to the upstart Houston Rockets, who had center Moses Malone and forward Cedric Maxwell on their roster. The Rockets had the poorest league record of any team making the playoffs, and the Celtics had the best. Still, it took Bird and Company six games to do the trick.

Despite a close, well-played series, the best moment might have come in Game 1 when Bird made what Red Auerbach called "the greatest play I've ever seen." Missing an 18-foot jumper from the right wing, Bird nailed the rebound as it came high off the rim, shifted the ball from his right to his left hand, and flipped in a follow-up shot that went down as he sprawled to the floor!

Boston came right back to lead the Eastern Conference in 1981-82, again with the best record in the league. Fans and sportswriters were already talking about a Bird vs. Magic series. But this time in the semifinals they ran into a wall called Philadelphia. Maybe Boston was lucky to lose, because the Sixers in turn ran into a wall called the Lakers. They lost the title 4-2, as Magic ran off with the MVP award. Los Angeles had its second title in three years.

Things were looking glum for Philadelphia. They had not won an NBA Championship in 16 years. 1982-83 would be their year. The Milwaukee Bucks swept Boston in the playoffs, then lost 4-1 to Dr. J and the Sixers. With Moses Malone now wearing a Philadelphia uniform, the Sixers were unbeatable. Malone had an MVP series, outmuscling Abdul-Jabbar. The Sixers swept the Lakers 4-0, and finally brought the trophy back to their home town.

As good as they were, the Sixers could not repeat in 1983-84. It had been a long time since any team had won back-to-back championships. Malone had an off year, and the Sixers were upset by the New Jersey Nets in the first round of the playoffs. Boston saw their chance and went for it, finding themselves pitted against the Lakers in the finals. It was the first time the two teams had met since the days of Bill Russell.

And what a series it was! Abdul-Jabbar and the fast-breaking, playmaking Magic taking on Bird and the

Los Angeles' Kareem Abdul-Jabbar attempts to block the shot of Philadelphia's Moses Malone (2) during the first game of the 76ers vs. Lakers NBA finals. L.A. won in six games.

outside-shooting Celtics, who played a more physical game. It was hyped as a rematch of the Magic vs. Bird 1979 NCAA Championship series when these two superstars first met on the court (Johnson's Michigan State beat Bird's Indiana State 75-64).

The Lakers took Games 1 and 3 easily, losing Games 2 and 4 in overtime. With the series knotted 2-2, the Celtics took Game 5, 121-103. The Lakers were struggling. Game after game, Abdul-Jabbar suffered migraine headaches. Through the first three quarters of Game 6, Boston's doggedness prevailed. But then the Lakers woke up, put on a shooting display, and evened the series at three games apiece. The situation was tense. Game 4 had already seen a bench-emptying scuffle between the Lakers' Kurt Rambis and Boston's Kevin McHale. But the Lakers just could not do it. Bird was everywhere, averaging 27 points and 11 rebounds per game and winning the MVP. He helped the Celtics take the prize, 111-102, before the largest television audience in NBA history. The Lakers had yet to win a championship against Boston.

Showtime

The 1984-85 season repeated this championship battle. The Lakers were routed 148-114 in the opening game, then bounced back to take a 2-1 lead in the series. It was another bruising series, with the Lakers forced to match Boston's physical style. By now the Laker-Celtic rivalry had become a real grudge match.

Despite all the pushing and the occasional punch, some dazzling basketball got played. In that Game 1 Boston rout, Scott Wedman came off the bench for the Celtics and canned his first 11 shots, four of them three-pointers! In Game 2 Abdul-Jabbar swished a "skyhook"—his special hook shot—that made him the all-time playoff scorer with 4,458 points. In fact, the 38-

year-old center was having a tremendous series, an MVP series. With Magic providing 14 points, 14 assists and 10 rebounds in the sixth and final game, and new Laker star James Worthy shooting 28 points, the Lakers finally had Boston in the bag, winning 111-100.

With Bird winning his third-straight regular season MVP, the Celtics roared back in 1985-86. The Lakers, however, shocked everyone by losing to Houston in the semifinals, 4-1. The Rockets, led by Hakeem Olajuwon, could not stop Bird and the Celtics. As Olajuwon put it, describing Bird and his MVP performance: "He's the greatest player I've ever seen." It had been Bird's year. In Game 6, Bird shot three-pointers as if they were lay-ups. He finished with 29 points, 11 rebounds, 12 assists, and 3 steals. Spectacular by anybody else's standards—average for Bird. Including the playoffs, the Celtics set an 82-game record for wins, taking the crown in six games.

Houston might have shown signs of becoming the "team of the future" that year, but in June 1987 it was the Lakers vs. the Celtics for the NBA crown. Bird led the Celts to another winning season, but Magic took the year's MVP. Rolling over Boston in the first two games of the finals, Los Angeles started talking "sweep." No way. Bird scored 30 points in Game 3, and the Celts were back in it, winning two out of three at home. They returned to Los Angeles, down 3-2, looking for back-to-back championships, but it was not to be. With seconds remaining, Bird canned a three-pointer that put the Celts up by two. Then mighty Kareem dropped a free throw and Magic swished a skyhook of his own, sinking the Celtics for good. Final score: 106-93. L.A. had done it again, beating Boston 4-2.

Fans were starting to wonder if they would ever see anybody else in the NBA Championship besides Boston and Los Angeles. Actually, other teams were in

In the 1980s forward Larry Bird brought back the championship fever to Boston Garden.

Magic Johnson earned the Most Valuable Player award in three NBA Championships during the 1980s.

the wings—including Utah, Dallas, and Chicago—getting ready for their big moment. But somebody forgot to tell the Lakers. Boston, once again finishing first after a 29.9-point per game year by Bird, lost out to Detroit in the semifinals. In Los Angeles, Coach Pat Riley was talking back-to-back Laker championships.

By now, the Lakers were known as the team of the 1980s, and not even the Pistons' Isiah Thomas could do anything about it. He tried, though. After all those NBA

The skyhook of Kareem Abdul-Jabbar made him the game's all-time leading scorer, and helped the Lakers win five championships.

Championship matches between Boston and Los Angeles, Detroit brought some "run-and-gun" flash to the finals. Detroit split the first two games in Los Angeles, winning 105-93 and then losing 108-96, before taking two out of three on their home court. Down 3-2, and in the face of a 43-point burst from Thomas, the Lakers managed to tie the series at 3-3 in a rousing 103-102 ball game. Then, in the seventh and final game, Laker James Worthy pumped in 36 points, nabbed 16 rebounds, and won the MVP going away. The Lakers had fulfilled their coach's prediction. They were the first team to repeat since 1969, and the first team to win three straight seven-game playoff series, having dumped Utah, Dallas, and Detroit.

Abdul-Jabbar Retires

The end of the decade. After the last game of the finals, Kareem Abdul-Jabbar would retire, ending not only the decade but perhaps the finest career in basketball history. And although many hoped the Lakers would make a retirement present of three straight NBA crowns to their big center, Detroit did not. The Pistons had never won an NBA Championship. After all was said and done, it seemed natural and fitting that Isiah Thomas, Joe Dumars, Vinnie Johnson, and Bill Laimbeer should close the decade with a 4-0 sweep of the Lakers. Magic was on the sidelines with a pulled hamstring muscle, and Abdul-Jabbar alone could not contain the Piston's back court. Dumars averaged 27 points per game, capturing the MVP, as Detroit won their first title.

The decade that belonged to Los Angeles and Boston had come to an end. A legend named Kareem was gone from the game. It was time for a new decade and some fresh, new faces.

Isiah Thomas ran the floor game for the Detroit Pistons, winners of their second NBA title in 1990.

The 1990s

In June 1990 the Detroit Pistons made it to the finals for the third straight year, and there was some whispering around the league about another dynasty. The Portland Trail Blazers, with all-star Clyde Drexler at the helm, beat the Phoenix Suns in a semifinal shootout. The Pistons were looking to repeat as champions, and the Blazers were determined to prevent it.

They split the first two games in Detroit, the Pistons coming out on top in a closely fought 106-99 opener, and the Blazers fought back to even the series with a 106-105 overtime victory. The Piston's back-court duo of Isiah Thomas and Joe Dumars combined for a 121-106 rout in Game 3, but all the talk was about their teammate and center, Bill Laimbeer. Dubbed "Bad Boy," Laimbeer hustled and muscled his team up and down the court, leaving Portland to complain about Detroit's aggressiveness.

Laimbeer distracted the Portland

NBA Trivia

Q: *Given a minimum of 25 games, who holds the highest lifetime average for points-per-playoff game?*
A: *Michael Jordan, with a 35.4 point average.*

Q: *Who holds the record for most rebounds in playoff action?*
A: *Bill Russell, with 4,104.*

Q: *Who holds the record for the highest rebounds-per-playoff game?*
A: *Bill Russell, with a 24.9 average.*

No team can win a championship without great defense,
something Detroit's Dennis Rodman has in abundance.

team to the point of defeat. Then, with the Pistons up 3-1, Thomas took over to finish them off. Besides holding the Blazers' fast-break tempo to a crawl, Thomas hit three-point jumpers and was deadly inside, twisting through the key for some easy lay-ups. Game 5 ended the series in Portland, with Detroit holding onto a heartstopping 92-90 edge at the buzzer. Averaging 27.6 points, 7 assists and 5.2 rebounds per game, Thomas was voted MVP.

With back-to-back NBA championships under their belt, Detroit players were calling themselves one of the "best teams in the history of basketball," comparing themselves to the Lakers and Celtics of yesteryear. But Detroit had some serious rivalry in their own division: The Chicago Bulls and Michael Jordan.

With Jordan's one-man show leading the Bulls, they blew away the Pistons in the semifinals. The stage was set for one of the most promising matchups in NBA Championship history: Michael Jordan vs. Magic Johnson. Los Angeles, having overcome the loss of Kareem Abdul-Jabbar, seemed ready to make the 1990s another "Decade of the Lakers."

As captains representing their teams at mid-court, the "MJ Twins" shook hands for Game 1 in Chicago. The game lived up to its hype. Jordan was everywhere at once, scoring 36 points, snagging 8 rebounds, and passing for 12 assists. Meanwhile, Magic—double-teamed by the Bulls—passed again and again, letting his teammates score enough to win 93-91.

It looked like L.A.'s team play would make a mess of Jordan's one-man show. But Jordan came roaring back, diving into the stands, sinking three-pointers, and swooping up the middle. When the dust had settled, the Bulls were in command of the series, 3-1. Magic's teammates seemed to collapse around him. James Worthy had a badly sprained ankle, and Byron Scott

Jordan takes a free throw shot during the Bulls' first NBA Championship victory.

and Terry Teagle could not buy a bucket. Meanwhile, the Bulls proved they were more than a one-man team after all. Forwards Scottie Pippen and Horace Grant came into their own, as did guards John Paxson and center Bill Cartwright. After four games Jordan averaged 31.5 points, 7.3 rebounds, 11.8 assists, and 2.3 steals to Johnson's 19.3 points, 7.3 rebounds, 10.5 assists, and 1.3 steals.

The Bulls were turning the Lakers inside out. They rolled over the Lakers 107-86 in Game 2. A 14-foot jumper by Jordan with 3.4 seconds left sent Game 3 into overtime, with the Bulls emerging victorious, 104-96. Again, Jordan could not miss in Game 4, scoring all over the court, and the Lakers went down 97-82 at home.

They would lose the championship at home, too. Jordan was dazzling in Game 5 at the Forum— offensively and defensively. This was the eleventh five-game series in NBA history, and Jordan set records for assists (57) and steals (14). Best of all, Chicago's first championship crown was a team effort. Pippen contributed a game-high 32 points to the Bulls' 108-101 victory. Paxson shot a remarkable .653 for the series. Grant averaged a more than respectable 14.6 points per game, on .627 shooting. It was Jordan's show, but he could not have done it without his teammates. No longer branded as a one-man team, the Bulls were fast becoming everyone's choice as the "Team of the 1990s." Only time will tell.

One team to watch for in future finals is the Portland Trail Blazers, with hot-shooting guard Clyde Drexler.

All-Time NBA Leaders

Year	Winner	Series	Loser
1947	Philadelphia Warriors	4-1	Chicago Stags
1948	Baltimore Bullets	4-2	Philadelphia Warriors
1949	Minnesota Lakers	4-2	Washington Capitols
1950	Minnesota Lakers	4-2	Syracuse
1951	Rochester	4-3	New York
1952	Minnesota Lakers	4-3	New York
1953	Minnesota Lakers	4-1	New York
1954	Minnesota Lakers	4-3	Syracuse
1955	Syracuse	4-3	Ft. Wayne Pistons
1956	Philadelphia Warriors	4-1	Ft. Wayne Pistons
1957	Boston	4-3	St. Louis Hawks
1958	St. Louis Hawks	4-2	Boston
1959	Boston	4-0	Minnesota Lakers
1960	Boston	4-3	St. Louis Hawks
1961	Boston	4-1	St. Louis Hawks
1962	Boston	4-3	Los Angeles Lakers
1963	Boston	4-2	Los Angeles Lakers
1964	Boston	4-1	S. Francisco Warriors
1965	Boston	4-1	Los Angeles Lakers
1966	Boston	4-3	Los Angeles Lakers
1967	Philadelphia Warriors	4-2	S. Francisco Warriors
1968	Boston	4-2	Los Angeles Lakers
1969	Boston	4-3	Los Angeles Lakers

All-Time NBA Leaders

Year	Winner	Series	Loser
1970	New York	4-3	Los Angeles Lakers
1971	Milwaukee	4-0	Baltimore Bullets
1972	Los Angeles Lakers	4-1	New York
1973	New York	4-1	Los Angeles Lakers
1974	Boston	4-3	Milwaukee
1975	Golden State Warriors	4-0	Washington Bullets
1976	Boston	4-2	Phoenix
1977	Portland	4-2	Philadelphia 76ers
1978	Washington Bullets	4-3	Seattle
1979	Seattle	4-1	Washington Bullets
1980	Los Angeles Lakers	4-2	Philadelphia 76ers
1981	Boston	4-2	Houston
1982	Los Angeles Lakers	4-2	Philadelphia 76ers
1983	Philadelphia 76ers	4-0	Los Angeles Lakers
1984	Boston	4-3	Los Angeles Lakers
1985	Los Angeles Lakers	4-2	Boston
1986	Boston	4-2	Houston
1987	Los Angeles Lakers	4-2	Boston
1988	Los Angeles Lakers	4-3	Detroit Pistons
1989	Detroit Pistons	4-0	Los Angeles Lakers
1990	Detroit Pistons	4-1	Portland
1991	Chicago	4-1	Los Angeles Lakers

Glossary

FREE THROW. Any uninhibited shot made from the foul line, after a player or team has been called for a shooting foul.

JUMP SHOT. A shot made as a player leaps in the air, releasing the ball at the height of his jump.

LAY-UP. An inside shot, usually made as a player drives to the basket, lightly bouncing the ball off of the backboard and into the hoop. Also called a *lay-in*.

OVERTIME. An extra period, after regulation play ends in a tie.

REBOUND. To grab the ball off either the offensive backboard or the defensive backboard.

SKYHOOK. A high, arching hook shot invented and perfected by Kareem Abdul-Jabbar.

Bibliography

Books

Dolan, Edward F., Jr. *Great Moments in the NBA Championships*. New York: Franklin Watts, 1982.

Heeren, Dave. *The Basketball Abstract*. Englewood Cliffs: Prentice-Hall, 1988.

Hill, Bob, and Randall Baron. *The Amazing Basketball Book*. Louisville: Devyn Press, 1987.

Hollander, Zander. *Basketball's Greatest Games*. Englewood Cliffs: Prentice-Hall, 1978.

Neft, David S., and Richard M. Cohen. *The Sports Encyclopedia: Pro Basketball*. New York: St. Martin's Press, 1989.

Rosen, Charles. *God, Man and Basketball Jones*. New York: Holt, Rinehart and Winston, 1979.

Periodicals

Carry, Peter. "Hey, Look, Ma! Only One Hand." *Sports Illustrated*, May 10, 1971: 26.

Carry, Peter. "Swish and They're In." *Sports Illustrated*, May 15, 1972: 26.

Carry, Peter. "A Matter of Celtic Pride." *Sports Illustrated*, May 20, 1974: 22.

Cotton, Anthony. "They Took It Down to the Wire." *Sports Illustrated*, June 18, 1984: 22.

Deford, Frank. "Two Seconds Stretch for First." *Sports Illustrated*, April 20, 1968: 24.

Deford, Frank. "East Is Knicks but West Is West." *Sports Illustrated*, May 11, 1970: 30.

Deford, Frank. "In for Two Plus the Title." *Sports Illustrated*, May 18, 1970: 14.

Kirkpatrick, Curry. "All for One Sure Beats One for All." *Sports Illustrated*, June 13, 1977: 30.

McCallum, Jack. "Your Ball, L.A." *Sports Illustrated*, June 22, 1982: 14.

McCallum, Jack. "The Final Agenda." *Sports Illustrated*, June 12, 1989: 28.

McCallum, Jack. "The Villain Was a Hero." *Sports Illustrated*, June 18, 1990: 26.

McCallum, Jack. "Thorns in the Roses." *Sports Illustrated*, June 25, 1990: 32.

McCallum, Jack: "Shining Moment." *Sports Illustrated*, June 24, 1991: 38.

McDermott, Barry. "Suns Worship Back in Fashion." *Sports Illustrated*, June 7, 1976: 20.

McDermott, Barry. "Call Them Champs Again." *Sports Illustrated*, June 14, 1976: 20.

Newman, Bruce. "Thou Shalt Rejoice, Said Moses." *Sports Illustrated*, June 13, 1983: 40.

Newman, Bruce. "Together at Center Stage." *Sports Illustrated*, June 4, 1984: 32.

Newman, Bruce. "Pushed to the Brink." *Sports Illustrated*, June19, 1989: 20.

Newman, Bruce. "Man in the Slow Lane." *Sports Illustrated*, June 26, 1989: 28.

Papenek, John. "It Was Seattle, Handily." *Sports Illustrated*, June 11, 1979: 16.

Papenek, John. "Arms and the Man." *Sports Illustrated*, May 26, 1980: 19.

Papenek, John. "So Far, So Miraculous." *Sports Illustrated*, May 18, 1981: 26.

Papenek, John. "Once More, with a Lot of Feeling." *Sports Illustrated*, May 25, 1981: 34.

Putnam, Pat. "The Warriors Were Bulletproof." *Sports Illustrated*, June 2, 1975: 20.

Wolff, Alexander. "The 'Movie Stars' Changed Their Act." *Sports Illustrated*, June 10, 1985: 36.

Photo Credits

ALLSPORT USA: 4, 40 (J. Daniel); 32, 38, 33 (Rick Stewart); 34 (Mike Powell); 36, 42 (Joe Patronite)

Basketball Hall of Fame: 7, 10 (Edward J. and Gena G. Hickox Library)

Bettman Archive: 16, 24, 29

Wide World Photos: 13, 14, 18, 21, 26

Index

Abdul-Jabbar, Kareem, 5, 6, 8, 12, 21-22, 23, 25, 27, 28, 29, 30-31, 34, 35, 39

Alcindor, Lew, *see* Abdul-Jabbar, Kareem

Arnett, Dick, 19

Auerbach, Arnold "Red," 11, 12, 14, 15, 28

Barry, Rick, 6, 11, 18, 23

Baylor, Elgin, 13-15, 17, 19

Bird, Larry, 5, 27-28, 30, 31, 32, 33

Bradley, Bill, 19

Cartwright, Bill, 41

Chamberlain, Wilt, 6, 15-17, 19, 20, 22

Chenier, Phil, 6

Clifton, Nat, 9

Coleman, Jack, 9

Cooper, Michael, 11

Cousy, Bob, 11, 12, 14, 15

Cowens, Dave, 6, 22

Davies, Bob, 9

DeBusschere, Dave, 18, 19

Drexler, Clyde, 37

Dumars, Joe, 35, 37

Erving, Julius "Dr. J," 6, 26, 27, 28

Frazier, Walt, 19, 20, 21

Grant, Horace, 41

Hannum, Alex, 12

Havlicek, John, 10, 11, 17, 22-23

Hawkins, Tommy, 15

Hayes, Elvin, 6

Heard, Garfield, 25

Heinsohn, Tom, 11, 12

Holzman, Red, 9, 19

Johnson, Magic, 4, 5, 11, 25, 27, 28, 30, 31, 33, 39

Johnson, Vinnie, 35

Jones, Sam, 15

Jordan, Michael, 4, 5, 37, 39, 40, 41

Laimbeer, Bill, 35, 37-38

Malone, Moses, 27, 28, 29

Maxwell, Cedric, 27

McHale, Kevin, 30

Mikan, George, 8-9, 11, 13

Naismith, James A., 6-7

Olajuwon, Hakeem, 31

Paxson, John, 41

Pettit, Bob, 12

Pippen, Scottie, 41

Rambis, Kurt, 30

Reed, Willis, 6, 19, 20

Robertson, Oscar, 21-22

Rodman, Dennis, 38

Russell, Bill, 6, 11, 12, 15-17, 22, 28, 37

Scott, Byron, 39-41

Selvy, Frank, 15

Sharman, Bill, 12

Teagle, Terry, 41

Thomas, Isiah, 33-35, 36, 37, 39

Tresvant, John, 20

Unseld, Wes, 6

Walton, Bill, 6, 24, 25

Wedman, Scott, 30

West, Jerry, 5, 17, 19, 20, 22

Worthy, James, 31, 35, 39